Countries Around the World

Vietnam

Charlotte Guillain

www.raintreepublishers.co.uk
Visit our website to find out more information about Raintree books.

To order:

☎ Phone 0845 6044371

📄 Fax +44 (0) 1865 312263

🖳 Email myorders@raintreepublishers.co.uk

Customers from outside the UK please telephone +44 1865 312262

Raintree is an imprint of Capstone Global Library Limited, a company incorporated in England and Wales having its registered office at 7 Pilgrim Street, London, EC4V 6LB – Registered company number: 6695582

Edited by Abby Colich and Claire Throp
Designed by Ryan Frieson and Steven Mead
Original illustrations © Capstone Global Library Ltd, 2012
Illustrated by Oxford Designers & Illustrators
Picture research by Ruth Blair
Originated by Capstone Global Library Ltd
Printed in China by China Translation and Printing Services

ISBN 978 1 406 23552 4
15 14 13 12 11
10 9 8 7 6 5 4 3 2 1

British Library Cataloguing in Publication Data
Guillain, Charlotte.
Vietnam. -- (Countries around the world)
959.7'044-dc22
A full catalogue record for this book is available from the British Library.

Acknowledgements

We would like to thank the following for permission to reproduce photographs: © Capstone Global Library Ltd p. 33 (Gareth Boden); Alamy pp. 11 (© Spencer Grant), 22 (© Peter Arnold, Inc.); Corbis pp. 10 (© William James Warren/Science Faction), 12 (© Jacques Pavlovsky/Sygma), 34 (© Christophe Boisvieux), 39 (© Bettmann); Dreamstime.com pp. 13 (© Kelvinett), 18 (© Chrispyphoto), 35 (© Louise Rivard), 37 (© Xiaobin Qiu); Getty Images p. 31 (Cameron Spencer); iStockphoto pp. 20 (© Windzepher), 24 (© YinYang), 30 (© John Kirk); Photolibrary p. 6 (Steve Vidler/Imagestate); Shutterstock pp. 5 (© Guillermo Garcia), 9 (© Itinerant Lens), 15 (© Philip Date), 16 (© Muellek Josef), 19 (© beboy), 21 (© Trinh Le Nguyen), 23 (© Marc van Vuren), 27 (© zeber), 29 (© Selfiy), 46 (© Fotogroove).

Cover photograph of a boat on the river reproduced with permission of iStockphoto (© syolacan).

We would like to thank Quang Phu Van for his invaluable help in the preparation of this book.

Every effort has been made to contact copyright holders of any material reproduced in this book. Any omissions will be rectified in subsequent printings if notice is given to the publisher.

Contents

Some words in the book are in bold, **like this**. You can find out what they mean by looking in the glossary.

Introducing Vietnam

What do you know about Vietnam? You may have only heard about the wars fought there. You may have eaten delicious Vietnamese food. But do you know where Vietnam is located in the world? What do you know about the country's fascinating history and **culture**? What does the landscape look like, and what are the main cities like?

Unique nation

Vietnam is a beautiful country that has recovered from the destruction of war to become an exciting nation. It lies in the eastern part of Southeast Asia. It covers an area of 331,210 square kilometres (127,880 square miles), a bit bigger than the UK and Ireland. Hanoi and Ho Chi Minh City are lively, thriving **urban** areas. But much of Vietnam is countryside, filled with stunning forests, coastlines, mountains, and **paddy fields**. Some of the world's rarest animals live in Vietnam.

Lands reunited

Vietnam has been invaded, turned into a **colony**, and divided over the centuries. The effects of this history can still be found today. But the Vietnamese people have managed to develop their own unique culture and customs. They are proud to show their country to visitors, who receive a warm welcome. Read on to find out more about this fascinating country and its people.

How to say...

Here are some useful Vietnamese greetings:

Hello	*Xin chào*	(sin chow)
Goodbye	*Tạm biệt*	(tam bee-et)
How are you?	*Có khỏe không?*	(kaw kair kong)
Please	*Làm on*	(lam ern)
Thank you	*Cám on*	(cam ern)

Halong Bay is famous for its stunning natural beauty.

History: conflict and communism

For thousands of years, humans have lived in the lands that now make up Vietnam. Groups of people in the northern Red River **Delta** area grew rice around 4,000 years ago. This led to a system of **irrigation** and an ordered society, called the kingdom of Van Lang. Its people, the Lac Viet, made bronze tools and had their own unique **culture**.

Chinese expansion and Indian influence

By 111 BC Chinese emperors of the Han **Dynasty** (206 BC–AD 220) ruled the Red River Delta region. China controlled the area for 1,000 years. As a result, Vietnamese society and culture became heavily influenced by China.

Today, tourists visit the ruined temples from the Kingdom of Champa.

THE TRUNG SISTERS (UNKNOWN–AD 43)

Sisters Trung Trac and Trung Nhi led a rebellion in AD 39 against the Chinese, and they became the first rulers of Vietnam. Their reign as queens was short-lived, however, as better-organized Chinese troops beat them in AD 43. Rather than face defeat, the sisters drowned themselves.

Meanwhile, southern regions were influenced by traders and settlers from India. The city-state of Funan was set up in the Mekong Delta, and it became an important centre for trade between India and China until the AD 400s. Later, the Champa Kingdom became powerful in what is now central Vietnam.

Independence

The people in the north fought against Chinese rule for hundreds of years. Finally, in 939 the rebel Ngo Quyen became ruler of an independent Vietnamese kingdom, named Nam Viet, in the northern region. Lands to the south also gradually became part of the country, which remained independent for almost 1,000 years.

This map shows where the Kingdom of Champa was in central Vietnam.

Revolution and unity

Vietnamese lands were unsettled by wars and instability for centuries. China was an ever-present threat, but the Vietnamese always resisted. The territory that makes up today's Vietnam was divided among a number of different ruling families who fought and took land from each other. Eventually, Nguyen Anh made himself emperor of a united Vietnam in 1802.

Europeans arrive

Portuguese traders arrived in the early 1500s, setting up trading centres and ports. They used these places to take goods between Europe and China. In the mid-1800s, France sent a military force to Vietnam. France was trying to compete with Great Britain, which was expanding its own **empire**. In 1858 French ships took the port of Da Nang, and they eventually took control of the Mekong Delta. A forced **treaty** with the Vietnamese was signed, allowing France to rule various territories. By 1862 France had established a **colony** in the south.

French rule

By 1883, all of Vietnam was made part of a French **protectorate**. French officials ran the country, while Vietnamese people were given low-level jobs with little pay. France took all the useful resources and **exported** them. Life for most Vietnamese people became harder. As a result, a national **resistance** movement grew, opposing French rule.

Daily Life

More land was farmed under French rule, but very few Vietnamese people owned this land. Many poor people became **tenant farmers**, and they were forced to give as much as 60 per cent of their rice crop to landlords. Very few Vietnamese children went to school at all. Only the richest could go to school with French children.

Many buildings in Saigon, such as this cathedral, are a reminder of Vietnam's colonial past.

Communist resistance

By the 1920s, some Vietnamese groups resorted to violence. The French imprisoned and executed thousands of people. In 1930 a man called Ho Chi Minh set up the Vietnamese **Communist** Party. This later became the Viet Minh. In 1945 the Viet Minh led a successful **uprising**. As a result, the communist Democratic **Republic** of Vietnam was founded in northern Vietnam, led by Ho Chi Minh. Meanwhile, France kept control of southern Vietnam.

HO CHI MINH (1890-1969)

Ho Chi Minh was born Nguyen Tat Thanh. He lived in the United States, the United Kingdom, and France as a young man. He then returned to Vietnam to fight for independence. Ho Chi Minh led North Vietnam until his death in 1969. His image is still found all over Vietnam, and the southern city of Saigon was renamed Ho Chi Minh City after him.

More and more US troops arrived in Vietnam during the 1960s.

War

Conflict continued between the French and Vietnamese. Communist China offered support to the Viet Minh and northern Vietnam. This led the anti-communist United States to support France and the anti-communist south. In 1954 communist forces defeated the French. Vietnam was divided into communist North Vietnam, based in Hanoi, and anti-communist South Vietnam, based in Saigon.

Forces called the Viet Cong, supported by the communist north, fought against the anti-communist south. In response, the United States sent more and more military help to the south. These forces bombed the north for years. Meanwhile, fighting continued in the south. Thousands of US soldiers and millions of Vietnamese people were killed during the fighting.

Back in the United States, the war became increasingly unpopular. Huge anti-war demonstrations were held. Finally, US troops withdrew from Vietnam in 1973.

Reunion and refugees

Fighting continued between North Vietnam and South Vietnam. In April 1975, the communists overran Saigon in the south. In 1976, the north and south were joined as the **Socialist** Republic of Vietnam, based in Hanoi.

Many Vietnamese people were homeless, millions had been killed, and the **infrastructure** had been badly damaged. Floods, periods without rain, and bad harvests caused more problems. Hundreds of thousands of Vietnamese **refugees** began leaving the region by boat or on foot. The "Vietnamese boat people" then faced pirates, storms, starvation, and disease as they tried to reach a safe port.

Economic difficulties

In the following years, Vietnam faced conflict with many of its neighbours, including a short war with China and an invasion by Cambodia. Many **Western** countries refused to trade with Vietnam, so its **economy** suffered.

Vietnamese refugees crammed into overcrowded boats to try to reach freedom.

The government was forced to introduce changes, and in 1986 *doi moi* was introduced. This policy helped to modernize the economy and open up trade with the West. During the 1990s, relations improved with neighbours such as Cambodia and China. By the early 2000s, Vietnam's economy was growing.

Today, Vietnam is relatively settled. The worldwide financial crisis that began in 2008 has affected Vietnam badly. But life for most people is better than at any other time in the country's history.

These are the main ethnic groups in Vietnam.

Ethnic Groups

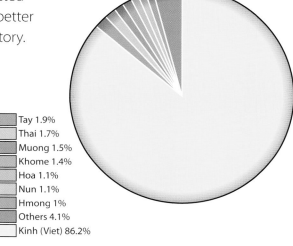

Tay 1.9%
Thai 1.7%
Muong 1.5%
Khome 1.4%
Hoa 1.1%
Nun 1.1%
Hmong 1%
Others 4.1%
Kinh (Viet) 86.2%

Ho Chi Minh City is a colourful, exciting city.

Regions and resources: Hanoi to Ho Chi Minh City

Vietnam is a long, thin country, stretching around 1,650 kilometres (1,025 miles) from north to south. It has 3,444 kilometres (2,140 miles) of coastline. It borders China to the north and Laos and Cambodia to the west. Vietnam's capital is Hanoi, which is in the northern part of the country.

In the south and north of Vietnam there are low, flat river **deltas**. Large **plateaus** lie in the centre, and there are mountains in the far north and northwest. Vietnam's climate is **tropical** in the south, while the cooler north experiences a rainy **monsoon** season from May to September and a warm, dry season the rest of the year.

Land height above sea level:

- Over 1500 m (4,921 ft.)
- Over 1000 m (3,281 ft.)
- Over 400 m (1,312 ft.)
- Over 200 m (656 ft.)
- Below 200 m (656 ft.)
- Country borders

0   125   250 kilometres

0   75   150 miles

This physical map of Vietnam shows the country's key natural features.

Farmers grow rice in paddy fields in the hills of northwest Vietnam.

Landscape and features

Vietnam's longest river is the Mekong River in the south. It flows through Southeast Asia for 4,350 kilometres (2,700 miles), starting in China and reaching the sea in Vietnam. The Mekong Delta's swampland and rice **paddy fields** make up a large part of southern Vietnam. This region often floods in the rainy season.

Further north, the central highlands lie around Da Lat and Kon Tum. The country's highest mountain, Fan Si Pan, is in the far north. Vietnam's largest lake is Ba Be, northwest of Hanoi. Important rivers in the north of the country are the Red River and the Black River.

How to say...

Here are some Vietnamese words for natural features:

River	*Sông*	(song)
Mountain	*Núi*	(noo-i)
Beach	*Bờ biển*	(ber bien)
Lake	*Hồ*	(ho)
Forest	*Rừng*	(rung)

Cities

There are five **municipalities** (*thành phố*) in Vietnam. These are Can Tho, Da Nang, Hanoi, Haiphong, and Ho Chi Minh City. Ho Chi Minh City, previously called Saigon, is the largest **urban** area, with a population of over seven million people. The city has developed and expanded quickly over the last few decades, and it is the heart of the country's **economy**. Hanoi is the centre of government. Can Tho is a vibrant trading centre in the Mekong Delta.

Daily Life

The Jarai people are an **ethnic minority** group living in the central highlands. Jarai women are treated with importance in this **culture**, deciding when to marry and passing their name on to their children.

The roads in Ho Chi Minh City are full of traffic.

Da Nang, in central Vietnam, is the country's most important port. Haiphong lies in the northeast, near China.

Regions

There are 58 **provinces** (*tinh*) in Vietnam. The northeastern province of Quang Ninh is home to the beautiful Ha Long Bay, with its stunning limestone peaks and islands jutting out of the sea. The central provinces lie at the country's narrowest part. Quang Nam is home to the Ba Na nature **reserve**, which is rich in wildlife and beautiful sandy beaches. The Son Doong Cave in Phong Nha-Ke Bang National Park and an underground river are found in Quang Binh Province. The provinces of the central highlands are full of mountain villages, waterfalls, and valleys. These areas are also important for agriculture (farming). Rice is grown in the southern delta region. The island of Phu Quoc, in Kien Giang Province, is a popular tourist destination.

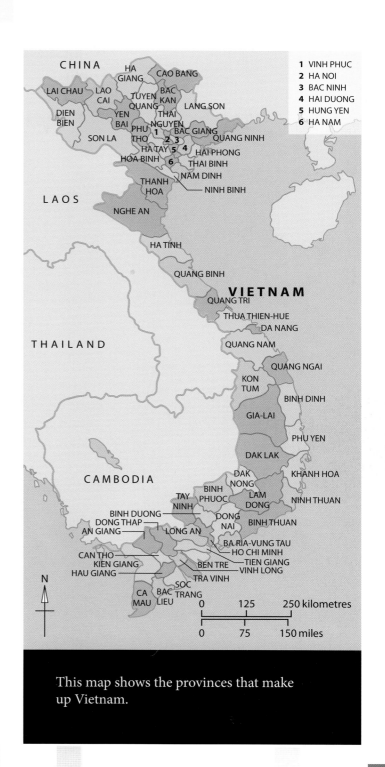

This map shows the provinces that make up Vietnam.

These women are working in a silk factory.

The economy

Like other **communist** countries, the Vietnamese government used to plan how to use all the country's resources. All businesses were owned by the government, which also decided what would be produced and sold. But in 1986, the government introduced some **free-market** ideas, such as letting people have their own businesses.

Today, the government and people decide together how to use the country's resources. These changes have led to growth in Vietnam's economy, and many people's standard of living has improved. However, the worldwide economic problems that began in 2008 hit Vietnam hard, as much of its income comes from **exports**. When other countries were hit by the crisis, they bought fewer items from Vietnam.

Industry and natural resources

Most factories in Vietnam produce goods for export. **Industry** began to change and expand rapidly when Vietnam joined the World Trade Organization in 2007. The biggest industry in Vietnam in terms of earning money is petroleum (oil). Other key industries are food processing, clothing manufacturing, machine building, mining, and the manufacture of steel, cement, fertilizers, glass, tyres, and paper.

Some important natural resources found in Vietnam include natural substances such as phosphates, coal, manganese, bauxite, chromate, oil and gas found off the coast, timber, and hydroelectric (water) power. Much of the land is good for farming, but farming has decreased as industry has expanded. Still, rice, seafood, and coffee remain some of Vietnam's biggest exports.

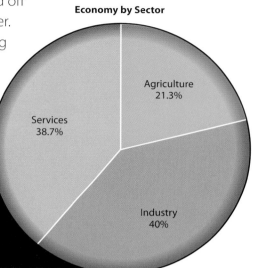

Economy by Sector

Agriculture
21.3%

Services
38.7%

Industry
40%

This chart shows how much of Vietnam's national income is produced by agriculture, industry, and services.

Many **rural** Vietnamese grow rice in paddy fields. It is hard work planting and harvesting the crop.

Wildlife: teak, tapir, and tiger

The douc langur monkey lives in the tree-tops in Vietnam's forests.

There are 30 national parks in Vietnam, covering 3 per cent of the country's land. Ba Be National Park in the north is made up of a **tropical** forest and limestone formations. Within its 8,000 hectares (19,768 acres) are caves and waterfalls, as well as many rare animals, such as Tonkin snub-nosed langurs. Yok Don National Park in the central highlands covers 115,000 hectares (284,170 acres). It is famous for its elephants and range of exotic birds. In Tram Chim National Park, in the Mekong **Delta**, there are many waterfowl. The Sarus crane can be seen there when the delta is not flooded.

How to say...

Here are some Vietnamese words for some of the country's wild animals:

Tiger	Hổ	(ho-ó)
Rhinoceros	*Con tê giác*	(kon tei zack)
Elephant	*Con voi*	(kon voy)
Leopard	*Con báo*	(kon bout)

Vietnam's forests

During the fighting with the United States in the 1960s and 1970s (see pages 10 and 11), much of Vietnam's forests were damaged or destroyed. Bombing and the use of chemicals did most of the damage. These chemicals, the most famous of which was called Agent Orange, made the leaves fall off trees in order to reveal hidden enemies. But the chemicals also poisoned and killed many Vietnamese people. These chemicals still cause problems today.

More recently, logging and the clearing of land for building and agriculture have led to the loss of forests. The government is trying to tackle this by planting new trees and encouraging communities to protect forests.

Timber logging is destroying many of Vietnam's natural habitats.

The rare Sumatran rhinoceros is the smallest type of rhinoceros in the world.

Vietnam's wildlife

In the central highlands of Vietnam, the wildlife includes elephants and tapirs. This region is also home to the Sumatran rhinoceros. People thought this animal had become extinct (died out) in the 1960s, but it was seen again in the 1990s. Other forest wildlife includes bears, tigers, and leopards. A type of wild oxen called a kouprey lives in Vietnam's forests, along with more common animals such as deer, wild pigs, porcupines, hares, and squirrels. In the trees, rhesus monkeys, gibbons, and langurs can be found. A number of new **species** have recently been discovered in Vietnam, including the deer-like saola, the tiger-striped pit viper, and a rough-coated tree frog.

Threatened species

Much of the unusual wildlife in Vietnam is **endangered**. Sumatran and Javan rhinoceros numbers have fallen, along with those of the tiger, Asian elephant, Chat Ba Island golden-headed langur, and kouprey. Many birds are also almost extinct.

Hunting, destruction of **habitats**, and the use of animals to make medicine all contribute to this decline in numbers. Vietnam is now trying to protect important areas. It is encouraging tourists to prevent further damage to important habitats.

The environment

Vietnam's **environment** faces a number of difficulties. Flooding is a problem in the Mekong Delta, and river water and sea water are often polluted. Overfishing along the coast has led to a drop in fish populations, and it has also damaged coral reefs. Meanwhile, the expansion of cities and **industry** means that many people are moving to **urban** areas. This causes overcrowding and pollution in large urban centres such as Ho Chi Minh City and Hanoi.

Flooding is a regular problem for people in Vietnam.

Infrastructure: politics and people

The **Socialist Republic** of Vietnam is a **communist** state with one political party. The president is **head of state**, supported by a vice president. A prime minister runs the government, helped by deputies and a cabinet of ministers. There are 493 seats in the National Assembly, with elections held every five years to decide on its membership. The National Assembly elects (chooses) the president. The president appoints the prime minister.

Ho Chi Minh is pictured on all Vietnamese banknotes.

The Vietnamese unit of **currency** is called the dong. There are coins and notes, with notes worth up to 500,000 dong. Since 2003, notes have been printed on plastic rather than paper, as this makes them stronger in the hot, humid climate.

Healthcare

Since the north and south reunified, Vietnam has benefited from improved heathcare across the country. But, more recently, the huge growth in Vietnam's population has put a strain on this system. Poorer people still struggle to afford healthcare, and hospitals can be overcrowded.

However, since 2000 some progress in public health has been made. For example, now 75 per cent of the population has access to clean water. There has also been a huge reduction in cases of the disease malaria. More doctors have been trained, and more infants are surviving birth and early childhood.

Unfortunately, at the same time, there has been an increase in the number of cases of tuberculosis and HIV/AIDS. It is important that the government continue to fund well-organized programmes to control and prevent these diseases from spreading.

Education

Parents in Vietnam expect their children to study hard and do their best. All children start primary school when they are six years old. They stay there for five years, before going on to middle school. Those who choose to continue their education then go to a secondary school.

YOUNG PEOPLE

Disabled children in Vietnam find it hard to go to school. But organizations are helping to address this problem. One project has trained 343 schools to use other pupils to support disabled children. For example, 10-year-old Lam is visually impaired, but friends help him to get to and from school, and they also help him with his lessons. The organization works to help people realize how much disabled people are capable of achieving.

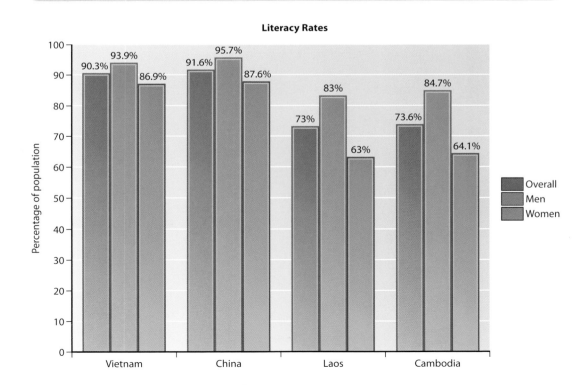

Literacy Rates

This bar chart compares literacy rates in Vietnam with neighbouring countries

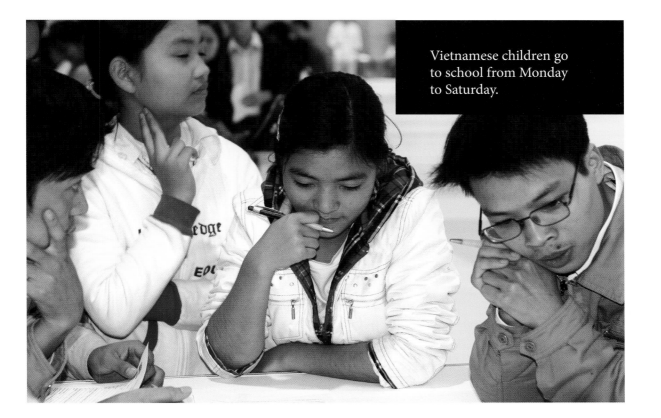

Vietnamese children go to school from Monday to Saturday.

Although education is required for nine years in Vietnam, many poorer children in **rural** areas stop going to school so they can work and earn money for their families. More than 40 per cent of Vietnam's children do not go to secondary school. Despite this, **literacy rates** in Vietnam are quite high, at 90.3 per cent. Only 9.7 per cent of the population goes on to university.

The school day

In Vietnam the school day is only around four hours long. In some larger schools, half the children come to school in the morning, while the rest come in the afternoon. The school year starts in September and ends in May. In many schools, children are responsible for keeping their classrooms clean.

Culture: water puppets and poetry

Vietnamese **culture** has been influenced and shaped by its history. The presence of both the Chinese and the French have affected some aspects of Vietnam's arts and **architecture**, but there is much that is unique to the country.

Music

The **communist** government of Vietnam used to stop people from listening to **Western** pop music, but today things are more relaxed. In cities, Western music is played everywhere. Young Vietnamese people also listen to their own local music.

YOUNG PEOPLE

Young people in Vietnam enjoy the reality television programme *Vietnam Idol*. Singers take part in a competition in which viewers vote for the best act. The female singer Uyên Linh won the competition in 2010.

Traditional music involves singing, often with one singer calling and the others responding. This singing is often performed without instruments. Other types of music are played along with theatre, such as *cai luong*. *Cai luong* is a type of drama based on Vietnamese folk songs and **classical** music. *Cai luong* means "renewed theatre". In the south, a cross between Western music and traditional folk singing features electric guitars.

Theatre

Many small theatre groups perform in Vietnam's cities. Theatre can include Western-style plays and traditional *cai luong*. The Vietnamese *cheo opera* is a form of theatre that began in ancient village festivals. A Chinese style of opera, called *hat tuong* in the north and *hat boi* in the south, is also popular.

Northern Vietnam is famous for its water puppetry (*mua roi nuoc*), which began with farmers using wooden puppets in rice **paddy fields**. Today, performances take place on a pool or pond. Puppeteers stand in the water, hidden behind a screen. Musicians and singers accompany the moving puppets.

Special theatres with pools have to be built for water puppetry shows.

This temple tower in central Vietnam was built in the 13th century.

Crafts and architecture

Different groups in Vietnam are known for their arts and crafts. Traditional Vietnamese crafts include **lacquerware** and woven blankets and clothes. In the central highlands, men weave baskets and mats. The Hmong people in the far north are known for their needlework.

There is a range of fascinating architecture in Vietnam, from the stilt houses in **ethnic minority** villages, to buildings dating back to when France ruled, to temples and **pagodas**.

Sports and leisure

Football is the most popular sport in Vietnam, in addition to volleyball, badminton, wrestling, cycling, chess, and dominoes. Vietnam has taken part in the Olympics since 1952, competing in martial arts, swimming, water sports, weight lifting, table tennis, and track events.

In their free time, many city people go for walks in parks and by lakes and rivers. Television is becoming more and more popular, and most people have access to a radio. The government controls all broadcasting and newspapers.

When the Internet was introduced to Vietnam in the late 1990s, the government tried to limit use by making it expensive. But by 2010, it was estimated that 27.1 per cent of the population was online, up from 0.3 per cent in 2000.

TRAN HIEU NGAN (BORN 1974)

Tran Hieu Ngan won a silver medal at the 2000 Olympics in women's tae kwon do. It was Vietnam's first-ever Olympic medal. The name Ngan actually means "silver" in Vietnamese!

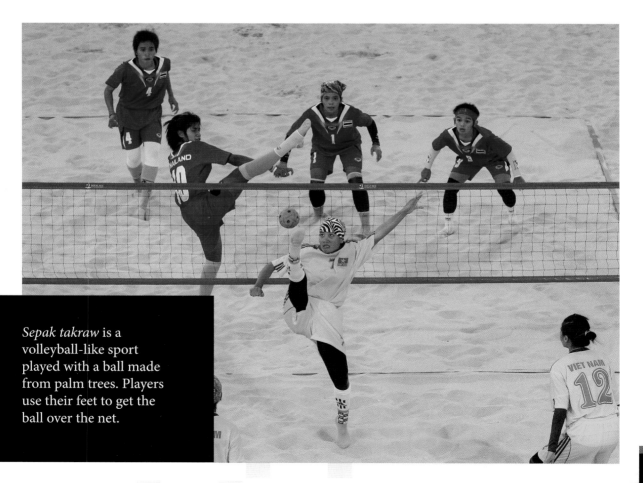

Sepak takraw is a volleyball-like sport played with a ball made from palm trees. Players use their feet to get the ball over the net.

Traditions and customs

Family is very important to most Vietnamese people, and they try to eat meals together as a family. People in **rural** areas tend to work from early morning until early evening, with a long rest during the hot midday. Most people wear modern clothes, but women still sometimes wear traditional clothing called *ao dai*. This includes a long, slit dress-like garment worn over trousers.

People take their shoes off before going into someone's home. They also think it is very rude to point the bottom of one's foot at someone! Many people bow slightly when they greet an older person.

The most important holiday in Vietnam is the lunar New Year's celebration known as *Tet*. This holiday falls between the last week of January and the third week of February, depending on the new moon. It is a time of feasting, visiting, and exchanging gifts. Vietnamese people also enjoy celebrating Christmas, Valentine's Day, and Halloween.

Food

Rice is the most important food in Vietnam. Vietnamese cooking is influenced by Chinese and other Southeast Asian cuisines. Common dishes include noodle soup with chicken or beef broth (*pho*), Vietnamese spring rolls (*cha gio*), and fermented fish sauce (*nuoc mam*). Many people in cities eat at street stalls and open-air restaurants.

Daily Life

Coffee is grown in Vietnam and is a very popular drink. People in the cities visit cafes or buy it from street sellers. It is often drunk with sweet condensed milk or made into iced coffee (*ca phe sua da*).

Caramelized chicken wings

Many Vietnamese dishes include honey or sugar. This makes the food sweet and sticky when it is cooked. When preparing this recipe, make sure an adult helps you to use the hob and hot oil.

Ingredients

8 chicken wings
2 tablespoons sesame oil
4 tablespoons honey
1 orange

4 tablespoons vegetable oil
salt and pepper

What to do

1. Sprinkle some salt and pepper over the chicken wings and put them on a plate.

2. Stir the sesame oil and honey together and brush this over the wings.

3. Peel off two long, wide strips of orange peel. Cut the peel into thin strips about the size of a matchstick.

4. Squeeze the juice from the orange.

5. Heat the oil in a frying pan over medium heat. Cook the chicken wings for about five minutes on each side.

6. Add the orange juice and strips of peel. Cover and simmer (at a gentle boil) for five minutes.

7. Take the lid off the pan and cook until the juices are thick. Cut into one of the chicken wings to check that the flesh is white, not pink.

8. Put the chicken wings onto a warm plate and spoon juices over them. Serve hot.

Vietnam today

Vietnam has come a long way since the war-torn years of the 1900s. Now it is a popular tourist destination thanks to its beautiful landscape and stunning beaches. The **communist** government has done much to improve the **economy**, which has grown and developed in recent years. In the 1980s, as many as 70 per cent of Vietnamese households lived in **poverty**. Today, only 12 per cent of the population lives in poverty.

The country's **infrastructure** has also been greatly improved, with better public transport links, healthcare, and educational opportunities available for most of the population.

Challenges ahead

Like many other countries, however, Vietnam has been facing economic challenges in the early 2000s. The worldwide financial crisis has affected the countries Vietnam trades with.

People burn perfumed sticks of incense during the New Year celebration known as *Tet*.

YOUNG PEOPLE

In recent years, young people have started moving from the countryside to the cities in Vietnam, which has resulted in a dramatic change in lifestyle. Traditional ways of life are being left behind as young people leave their families and live independent lives, often influenced by **Western** countries. But some Vietnamese people fear that rapid progress might come at the cost of long-held traditions and customs.

Many people now live in cities and only visit the countryside.

The Vietnamese government has also been criticized for its **human rights** record. People who question the government, and the lawyers who defend them, have been imprisoned. Many **ethnic minorities** are also unhappy with their treatment. Problems with the **environment** continue, and many animals and plants found in Vietnam are **endangered**.

Still, the future looks good for Vietnam, and the number of visitors going to this fascinating country is increasing each year. Why not find out more about this exciting and varied country and its people?

Fact file

Official name:	**Socialist Republic** of Vietnam
Language:	Vietnamese
Capital city:	Hanoi
Bordering countries:	China, Laos, Cambodia
Population:	90,549,390 (2011 est.)
Largest cities (populations):	Ho Chi Minh City (5,968,384) Hanoi (2,644,536) Haiphong (846,191)
System of government:	**Communist**
Religion:	Buddhist (9.3 per cent), Catholic (6.7 per cent), Hoa Hao (1.5 per cent), Cao Dai (1.1 per cent), Protestant (0.5 per cent), Muslim (0.1 per cent), none (80.8 per cent)
Birth rate:	17.29 births per 1,000
Life expectancy:	71.94 years (men, 69.48 years; women, 74.69 years)
Literacy rate:	90.3 per cent
Internet users:	24,269,083 (27.1 per cent of the population)
Area (total):	331,210 square kilometres (127,880 square miles)
Highest elevation:	Fan Si Pan, 3,144 metres (10,315 feet)
Lowest elevation:	South China Sea, 0 metres (0 feet)

Natural resources: Phosphates, coal, manganese, bauxite, chromate, offshore oil and gas deposits, timber, hydropower

Currency: Dong

Imports: Machinery and equipment, petroleum products, fertilizer, steel products, raw cotton, grain, cement, motorcycles

Exports: Crude oil, marine products, rice, coffee, rubber, tea, clothes, shoes

Hanoi is Vietnam's capital city.

National emblem: Red circle with a yellow star in the middle

Famous Vietnamese people:
Bui Xuan Phai (1920–1988), painter
Dinh Y Nhi (born 1967), artist
Ho Chi Minh (1890–1969), political leader
My Linh (born 1975), singer
Ngo Bao Chau (born 1972), mathematician
Nguyen Du (1766–1820), poet
Tran Hieu Ngan (born 1974), Olympic athlete

National holidays:

1 January	New Year's Day
late January/ mid-February	*Tet*, Vietnamese New Year for four days
30 April	Liberation of Saigon, 1975
1 May	International Labour Day
2 September	National Day

National anthem
"March to the Front"

Soldiers of Vietnam, we go forward,
With the one will to save our Fatherland
Our hurried steps are sounding on the long and arduous road
Our flag, red with the blood of victory, bears the spirit of our country
The distant rumbling of the guns mingles with our marching song.
The path to glory passes over the bodies of our foes.
Overcoming all hardships, together we build our resistance bases.
Ceaselessly for the people's cause we struggle,
Hastening to the battlefield!
Forward! All together advancing!
Our Vietnam is strong eternal.

Many people in Vietnam still call Ho Chi Minh "Uncle Ho".

Rural and Urban Populations

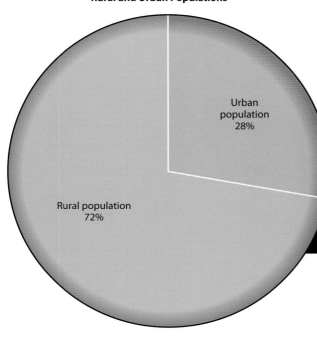

Urban population 28%

Rural population 72%

This pie chart shows what percentage of Vietnam's population lives in **rural** and **urban** areas.

Timeline

BC is short for "Before Christ". BC is added after a date and means that the date occurred before the birth of Jesus Christ, for example, 450 BC.

AD is short for *Anno Domini*, which is Latin for "in the year of our Lord". AD is added before a date and means that the date occurred after the birth of Jesus Christ, for example, AD 720.

BC

c. 2000	A Bronze Age **culture** develops around the Red River **Delta** in north Vietnam.
early 200s	The city-state of Funan trades with the Middle East and Europe.
mid-200s	China begins to take land in northern Vietnam.
111	The Chinese Han **Dynasty** brings the Red River Delta region into its **empire**.

AD

43	The Trung sisters kill themselves after three years of **resistance** to Chinese rule.
939	**Uprisings** against Chinese rule lead to Vietnamese independence.
1010	Hanoi becomes Vietnam's capital.
1407	China invades again.
1427	China is defeated by a united Vietnamese force.
1535	The Portuguese arrive at the port of Fai Fo, in central Vietnam.
1847	French ships attack Da Nang.
1858	A large French force is sent to Vietnam.
1862	France is in control of much of the Mekong Delta and some Vietnamese ports.

1883	All of Vietnam becomes a French **protectorate** that also includes Laos and Campuchia (modern-day Cambodia).
1939	World War II begins.
1945	World War II ends, and the Viet Minh lead an uprising. The **communist** Democratic **Republic** of Vietnam is founded in the north, led by Ho Chi Minh.
1954	France is defeated by communist forces. The Geneva Accords are signed, creating North Vietnam, based in Hanoi, and anti-communist South Vietnam, based in Saigon.
1960	North Vietnamese forces help communists in the south (the Viet Cong) fight against the South Vietnamese government. The United States sends aid to help the south.
1965	Fighting increases, with repeated US bombings of the north.
1968	Over 500,000 Americans are in Vietnam. In the Tet Offensive, thousands of communists attack cities in the south. Two thousand US soldiers, 2,300 South Vietnamese soldiers, and as many as 12,500 non-soldiers are killed. Attitudes in the United States begin to turn against the war.
1973	US troops withdraw from Vietnam, and US prisoners-of-war are released.
1975	Communist forces overrun Saigon. People start to leave Vietnam.
1976	The **Socialist** Republic of Vietnam is established, with its capital in Hanoi.
1986	The policy of *doi moi* is introduced to improve the **economy**.
1994	Trade is re-established with the United States.
2007	Vietnam joins the World Trade Organization.
2008	Vietnam is affected by the worldwide financial crisis.

Glossary

architecture design and style of buildings

classical artistic music, often played by an orchestra or piano

colony area ruled by another country

communist person or country that practises a social system in which all people share work and property

corruption act of breaking the law to acquire money or power

culture practices, beliefs, and traditions of a society

currency notes and coins accepted in return for goods and services

delta area at the mouth of a river, where it divides into branches

dynasty series of rulers from the same family or group

economy having to do with the money, industries, and jobs in a country

empire group of countries ruled by a single government or ruler

endangered in danger of dying out

environment natural world, including plants and animals

ethnic minority group of people of a different race or culture from the majority in a country

export to ship goods to other countries for sale or exchange

free-market type of economy in which the government is not involved in decisions about what a country produces

habitat environment where a plant or animal is found

head of state person who represents the country. Sometimes they are also the leader of the country.

human rights basic rights that most people believe everyone should have, for example access to food and shelter

industry organized business activity concerned with making, mining, processing, or constructing materials

infrastructure organizations and facilities, such as roads and hospitals

irrigation water supplied to land for growing crops

lacquerware decorative crafts coated in a shiny surface called lacquer

literacy rate number of people over the age of 15 who can read and write

monsoon season of heavy rain

municipality large district with its own local government, such as a city

paddy field land that is flooded so rice can be grown there

pagoda Asian temple, usually built as a layered tower with a curving roof

plateau large, flat area of highland

poverty extreme lack of money

protectorate country that is protected and partly controlled by another country

province specific region within a country

refugee person who has escaped from his or her home or country because of a war or disaster

republic independent country with a head of government who is not a king or queen

reserve area set aside to protect wildlife

resistance act of fighting against someone or something

rural to do with the countryside

socialist person or country that follows a political system in which there is common ownership of resources

species particular type of animal or plant

tenant farmer farmer who does not own the land he or she works on, but who pays rent to a landlord

treaty signed agreement between two or more countries

tropical hot and humid

uprising act of rebelling or rising up against authority

urban to do with cities and large towns

Western relating to European nations and other countries, such as the United States, Canada, and Australia, with similar political systems and cultures

Find out more

Books

Countries of the World: Vietnam, Edward Parker (Evans Brothers, 2005)
Escape from Saigon: How a Vietnam Orphan Became an American Boy,
 Andrea Warren (Farrar Straus Giroux, 2008)
The Atlas of People and Places, Philip Steele (Franklin Watts, 2008)
The Usborne Geography Encyclopedia, Jane Bingham et al (Usborne, 2010)
The Vietnam War, Katie Daynes (Usborne, 2008)
Vietnam (Fact Finders), Mary L. Englar (Capstone, 2007)

Websites

http://kids.nationalgeographic.com/kids/places/find/vietnam/
The National Geographic Kids website has lots of interesting images and facts
about Vietnam today, as well as a video of Ha Long Bay.

**http://news.bbc.co.uk/1/hi/world/asia-pacific/country_
profiles/1243338.stm**
Find out about Vietnam on the BBC's website.

www.who.int/countries/vnm/en/
The website of the World Health Organization (WHO) provides health
information concerning Vietnam.

http://whc.unesco.org/en/list
This page on the UNESCO website provides a list of all the World Heritage
sites in Vietnam and the rest of the world.

**https://www.cia.gov/library/publications/the-world-factbook/
index.html**
The World Factbook is a publication of the Central Intelligence Agency
(CIA) of the United States. It provides information on the history, people,
government, geography, and more on Vietnam and over 250 other countries.

Places to visit

If you are lucky enough to visit Vietnam, here are some of the places you could visit:

Cuc Phuong National Park

There is a primate rescue centre here, where you can see monkeys, gibbons, and other primates up close.

Kim Dong Theatre, Hanoi

Visit this theatre to see a water puppet performance by the Thang Long Water Puppet Troupe.

Ha Long Bay

Take a boat and explore the limestone pinnacles around the bay.

Further research

- Throughout the 1800s, in which other countries did France establish colonies?
- How and where did people in the United States protest against the Vietnam War?
- Find out more about one of the ethnic minorities living in Vietnam.
- What are Vietnam and other countries doing to protect endangered species such as the tiger?

You could find out more by visiting your local library, looking at the websites listed here, or visiting a museum or Vietnam itself.

Topic tools

You can use these topic tools for your school projects. Trace the flag and map on to a sheet of paper, using the thick black outlines to guide you, then colour in your pictures. Make sure you use the right colours for the flag!

The red background on the Vietnamese flag is a colour often used in communist countries. The five points of the yellow star are supposed to stand for the working people, the peasants, the military, intellectuals, and the middle classes in Vietnam.

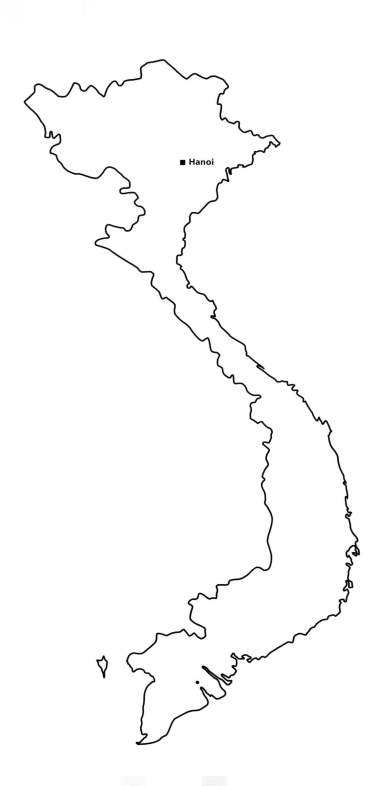

N

■ Hanoi

Index

Titles in the series

Afghanistan	978 1 406 22778 9	Japan	978 1 406 23548 7
Algeria	978 1 406 23561 6	Latvia	978 1 406 22795 6
Australia	978 1 406 23533 3	Liberia	978 1 406 23563 0
Brazil	978 1 406 22785 7	Libya	978 1 406 23564 7
Canada	978 1 406 23534 0	Lithuania	978 1 406 22796 3
Chile	978 1 406 22786 4	Mexico	978 1 406 22790 1
China	978 1 406 23547 0	Morocco	978 1 406 23565 4
Costa Rica	978 1 406 22787 1	New Zealand	978 1 406 23536 4
Cuba	978 1 406 22788 8	North Korea	978 1 406 23549 4
Czech Republic	978 1 406 22792 5	Pakistan	978 1 406 22782 6
Egypt	978 1 406 23562 3	Philippines	978 1 406 23550 0
England	978 1 406 22799 4	Poland	978 1 406 22797 0
Estonia	978 1 406 22793 2	Portugal	978 1 406 23578 4
France	978 1 406 22800 7	Russia	978 1 406 23579 1
Germany	978 1 406 22801 4	Scotland	978 1 406 22803 8
Greece	978 1 406 23575 3	South Africa	978 1 406 23537 1
Haiti	978 1 406 22789 5	South Korea	978 1 406 23551 7
Hungary	978 1 406 22794 9	Spain	978 1 406 23580 7
Iceland	978 1 406 23576 0	Tunisia	978 1 406 23566 1
India	978 1 406 22779 6	United States of America	978 1 406 23538 8
Iran	978 1 406 22780 2	Vietnam	978 1 406 23552 4
Iraq	978 1 406 22781 9	Wales	978 1 406 22804 5
Ireland	978 1 406 23577 7	Yemen	978 1 406 22783 3
Israel	978 1 406 23535 7		
Italy	978 1 406 22802 1		